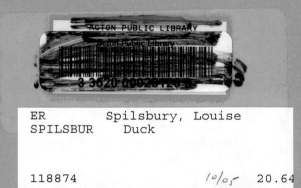

Life Cycles

Duck

Louise Spilsbury

Heinemann Library
Chicago, Illinois

Customer Service   888-454-2279

Visit our website at www.heinemannlibrary.com

Photo research by Maria Joannou and Debra Weatherly
Designed by Michelle Lisseter
Printed and bound in China by South China Printing Company

09 08 07 06 05
10 9 8 7 6 5 4 3 2 1

Library of Congress Cataloging-in-Publication Data
Spilsbury, Louise.
  Duck / Louise Spilsbury.
      p. cm. -- (Life cycles)
  Includes index.
  ISBN 1-4034-6771-4 (hard cover) -- ISBN 1-4034-6776-5 (paper back)
  1. Ducks--Life cycles--Juvenile literature. I. Title. II. Series.
  QL696.A52S655 2005
  598.4'1--dc22
                              2004020251

Acknowledgments
The author and publisher are grateful to the following for permission to reproduce copyright material: Alamy Images pp. 6, 22, 23 (beak); Ardea (John Daniels) pp. 5, 16; Bruce Coleman pp. 13 (Jane Burton), 17 (Jane Burton), 21 (Tero Niemi), 23 (webbed feet, Jane Burton; wings, Tero Niemi), back cover (duckling, Jane Burton); Corbis (George D. Lepp) p. 15; FLPA (D. Hosking) p. 14; Getty Images (Imagebank) p. 20; Nature Picture Library pp. 7 (Tom Vezo), 9 (Steven D. Miller), 12 (Mike Wilkes), 19 (Pete Oxford), back cover (eggs, Steven D. Miller); NHPA (Bill Coster) p. 8; Oxford Scientific Films pp. 4 (Martyn Chillmaid), 10 (Joaquin Gutierrez Acha), 23 (lay, Joaquin Gutierrez Acha); Papilio p. 11 (Robert Pickett); Science Photo Library (Bill Bachman/ Photo Researchers) p. 18

Cover photograph of a duck reproduced with permission of Corbis (Lynda Richardson)

Every effort has been made to contact copyright holders of any material reproduced in this book. Any omissions will be rectified in subsequent printings if notice is given to the publisher.

Many thanks to the teachers, library media specialists, reading instructors, and educational consultants who have helped develop the Read and Learn/Lee y aprende brand.

Contents

Some words are shown in bold, **like this.** You can find them in the picture glossary on page 23.

What Are Ducks?

These are ducks.

Ducks are birds.

Ducks live near water.

They start life inside an egg.

When Do Ducks Lay Eggs?

Female ducks lay eggs in the springtime.

They can make between five and twelve eggs.

Ducks look for safe places to lay their eggs.

Then, they make a **nest**.

What Are Nests?

A **nest** holds the eggs.

The mother duck makes a nest from leaves and grass.

The mother duck puts soft plants inside the nest.

Then she lays her eggs in the nest.

Who Looks After the Eggs?

The mother duck takes care of the eggs.

She sits on the eggs to keep them warm.

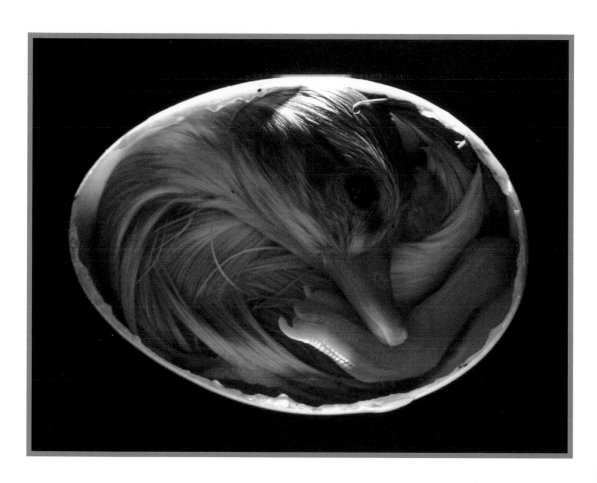

The mother duck sits on the eggs to keep them safe, too.

This also helps the babies inside to grow.

When Do Ducklings Come Out of the Eggs?

Baby ducks are called ducklings.

After a month the ducklings come out of the eggs.

Ducklings break open the eggs with their **beaks.**

They are covered in soft feathers.

When Do Ducklings Leave the Nest?

After the ducklings come out of their eggs, they are hungry.

They leave the **nest** to find food.

The ducklings follow their mother to find food.

They swim behind her in a line.

What Do Ducks Eat?

The mother duck shows the ducklings what to eat.

Ducks eat plants they find in the water.

Ducks have **webbed feet**.

Webbed feet help them to swim
and dive to get food.

How Do Ducklings Stay Safe?

The mother duck keeps the ducklings safe.

Big birds and fish try to eat ducklings.

Ducklings stay close to their mother.

She keeps them safe under her **wings**.

When Do Ducklings Learn To Fly?

Ducklings learn to fly when they are six weeks old.

They flap their **wings** to fly.

When ducklings grow up they leave their mother.

They fly away with other ducks.

Duck Diagram

wings

beak

feathers

webbed feet

Picture Glossary

beak
page 13
hard, pointed part of a bird's mouth

nest
pages 7, 8, 9, 14
place where a bird lays eggs

webbed feet
page 17
animal feet that have skin between the toes

wing
pages 19, 20
special arm covered in feathers that a bird uses to fly

Note to Parents and Teachers

Reading for information is an important part of a child's literacy development. Learning begins with a question about something. Help children think of themselves as investigators and researchers by encouraging their questions about the world around them. Each chapter in this book begins with a question. Read the question together. Look at the pictures. Talk about what you think the answer might be. Then read the text to find out if your predictions were correct. Think of other questions you could ask about the topic, and discuss where you might find the answers. Assist children in using the picture glossary and the index to practice new vocabulary and research skills.

Index